COLCHESTER
IN OLD PHOTOGRAPHS

EAST END OF HIGH STREET, June 1858. The half-ruined St Nicholas' Church sports its 'frying pan' clock. Note cobblestones, parked carts, men setting up a stall and the Victorian town hall in the distance. Some 97 years separate this picture from the last in the book, showing the same scene. (137T, 159.)

COLCHESTER
IN OLD PHOTOGRAPHS

—————COMPILED BY—————
ANDREW PHILLIPS

ALAN SUTTON
1989

Alan Sutton Publishing
Gloucester

First published 1989

British Library Cataloguing in Publication Data

Colchester in old photographs.
1. Essex. Colchester, history
I. Phillips, Andrew, 1938–
942.6'723

ISBN 0–86299–711–9

Typesetting and origination by
Alan Sutton Publishing
Printed in Great Britain by
Dotesios Printers Limited

CONTENTS

INTRODUCTION   6

1. IN THE BEGINNING   9

2. THE TOWN TO 1914: MAKING A LIVING   17

3. THE TOWN TO 1914: PUBLIC & SOCIAL   45

4. WAR & AFTER: 1914 – 1920   77

5. COLCHESTER BETWEEN THE WARS: 1920 – 1939   85

6. COLCHESTER AT WAR: 1939 – 46   133

7. POST-WAR COLCHESTER   151

   ACKNOWLEDGEMENTS   160

BOTTOM OF SCHEREGATE STEPS, February 1897. Snow, a milk cart and a lady passing. (106B.)

INTRODUCTION

Colchester boasts 2,000 years of history, but little of this was relevant when the camera arrived. In 1850 Colchester was a dozy market town with a great past and an unpromising future. This can be sensed in some of its early photographs.

Who took the first photograph in Colchester? As early as April 1845 Robert Hayward, an accountant by trade, offered daguerrotype portraits from a makeshift studio in his house in St John's Street, acting as agent for a London organization. But what of outdoor photography? This became more feasible for the amateur with the invention in 1850 of wet plate photography, using a glass negative.

Photographic experiment in Colchester owed much to the Gasworks. This is not as odd as it sounds: gas production, like photography, hinged on applied chemistry. In 1849 the Colchester works came into the hands of the ironmongers, Joslins. Working from a laboratory on Hythe Quay young John Joslin took many photographs in the early 1850s. Sadly, few have survived. The oldest known set of photographs of Colchester dates from the summer of 1858, taken by C.S. Brock who was, apparently, a young army officer whose family lived at St Mary's Terrace on Lexden Road.

These early photographs involved cumbersome equipment and a time exposure of several seconds. Anything that moved was a blur. Not till the 1880s did dry plate photography make possible exposures of a split second, showing people or vehicles on the move.

In few respects was Victorian Colchester better than today. This does not mean that lives were all unhappy. It does, however, warn us against photographic clichés. What looks picturesque may have been squalid; rural calm might, in reality, be quiet desperation. Colchester's 'Dutch Quarter' was not that romantic to people who lived there. I have in consequence tried to pick photographs showing Colchester 'warts and all', rather than the pretty and the picturesque which commercial postcards often suggest. I have also tried to include significant photographs, reflecting the town's development between 1850 and 1950.

Victorian progress was slow to reach Colchester but, after 1875, the town began to develop a genuine industrial base in engineering, boot and shoe manufacture and building. There were also several clothing factories, employing local women, many operating as outworkers from their own homes. As the population rose – dramatically after 1880 – the rich built lavish houses off the Lexden Road, while the poor crowded into slum properties in courtyards off Magdalen Street. New Town nearby was for the upwardly mobile.

The end of the century saw frenzied municipal progress: Jumbo the watertower, the Recreation Ground, the Castle Park, a Public Library, Sewage Works and, in the new century, trams, electricity and buses all run by the corporation. The lavish Edwardian town hall was really a secular cathedral, built to the glory of Colchester's long history. Civic ceremony was enhanced by a large military garrison; so was the business of beer houses and brothels. Colchester was nonetheless very godly: churches and chapels were full and a deal of social life revolved around them.

The first 50 years of the twentieth century were dominated by two World Wars. Both helped to revive (and disrupt) the town's new industries. Motor cars gradually replaced horses. The bypass of 1930–33 was one solution to this problem, as well as a civic response to unemployment. Colchester was not without an element of class conflict.

On the other hand it was a small town: an intermarried élite, a family feel to streets, neighbourhood schools and unity against hardship and the world outside – a mood enhanced by the collective spirit of the Second World War. Colchester in 1950 was still distinctly Essex. A rich local accent, a dry sense of humour perhaps masked a sense of inferiority to almighty London. Few foresaw the expansion that was to come.

In compiling this book I have depended heavily on two great collections of photographs. The first is held by the Colchester & Essex Museum, the product of 100 years of patient scholarship and conservation, a record of our town which otherwise would be lost. My second debt is to Colchester's two great newspapers, the *Essex County Standard* and the *Evening Gazette*, who for the past decade have regularly invited readers to allow their old photographs to be copied. As with the museum this has preserved a photographic record which might otherwise be unknown. To all who have sent in photographs I am indebted and have acknowledged elsewhere those which I have included. One positive consequence

GOSBECKS ROAD at the junction with Shrub End Road, opposite the Leather Bottle, 1920s. (132B.)

of compiling this book has been, through the good offices of Essex County Newspapers, the amalgamation of these two great collections. Finally I have had access to the large photograph collection in the County Library's Local Studies Library at Colchester. In all cases I have received great courtesy and much help, and would like to mention by name (alphabetically to avoid distinction) John Adams, Molly Blomfield, Paul Coverley, Sonny Cracknell, Jane Dansie, Derek Drew, Marcel Glover, Oliver Green, Peter Hills, Rita Hills, Laurie Honeyball, Tony Kidd, Jim Lee, Tony McGrath, Rosemary Oliver, Richard Shackle, Howard Walker and Martin Winter. I must also acknowledge the insights into everyday life supplied by the many contributors to the 'Colchester Recalled' oral history project.

Glancing through this book many of you will have old memories jogged. You may know more about a photograph than I do. There may be mistakes you can correct, stories you can tell or names you can supply. If so, we would like to hear from you. Please write to: Andrew Phillips, *Colchester in Old Photographs*, Museum Resources Centre, 14 Ryegate Road, Colchester. CO1 1YG.

Many photographs in this book invite comparisons. To help with this I have put in brackets after each caption the page number of any photographs which relate to the one you are looking at, followed by the letter T or B, which stand for top or bottom. Thus (35T, 109B) after a caption means compare this picture with the ones on the top of page 35 and the bottom of page 109.

In the Beginning: 1850–60

IS THIS COLCHESTER'S OLDEST SURVIVING OUTDOOR PHOTOGRAPH? Taken from the gasworks' chimney at the Hythe by John Joslin in autumn 1852. Across the river the *Margaret*, one of the last wooden ships built at the Hythe, lies on the stocks. Workmen are visible, the tide is in and corn ripens in the field behind Greenstead Road where, 81 years later, St Andrew's Avenue will run (104B). On the horizon, left of the haystacks, St Andrew's Church is shielded by trees. When this photograph was taken the Duke of Wellington was still alive.

THE HYTHE, 1852. A full view of the *Margaret*, built for the far east fruit trade. The stern is to the right, the ribs still under construction. Far right is Greenstead windmill. (19T.)

A PHOTOGRAPH TAKEN FROM THE IDENTICAL POSITION, 1856. The tide is out and timber yards (still there today) have replaced the defunct shipbuilding trade. (27B.)

WELCOME TO THE PRINCE

PRINCE ALBERT VISITED COLCHESTER, April 1856, to inspect the barracks, newly established at the close of the Crimean War. Coming from the railway station his cortège passed down a St Botolph's Street festooned with loyal decorations. (84B.)

QUEEN STREET, April 1856, looking towards Goody's shop where the War Memorial now stands (29T). A banner says: PRINCE ALBERT.

THE GERMAN LEGION, recruited during the Crimean War, in tents where now New Town stands, July 1856. Note the stacked rifles and, on the horizon, the camp church (61T) where, on one Sunday, 65 Germans married local girls to qualify for free passage to South Africa.

CROUCH STREET, looking east, opposite the end of Wellesley Road. A boy on the left is in Blue-coat uniform (52T); photographer unknown, date c. 1856. Most buildings are still there.

HIGH STREET, SATURDAY MORNING, May 1858, with hurdles up for sheep sales. Two men chatting, reduced to shadows. Behind: the Cups Hotel, the Victorian Town Hall, St Runwald's Church (23T). Beyond that the Middle Row is being demolished. The first of the photographs by C.S. Brock.

ST MARY'S-AT-THE-WALLS, June 1858, the 1714 church (rebuilt in 1872). The graveyard had been closed two years before, but burials in family vaults continued. Contemplating mortality was a Victorian hobby. They had lots of practice. This and the next three pictures are by C.S. Brock.

PUBLIC WELL IN ABBEY WALL at end of Mersea Road, June 1858 (117T). Posters on the wall advertise for 'hands' at Hyam's clothing factory (98). Colchester had 12 public wells, 438 private ones, many foul.

ST MARY'S TERRACE, LEXDEN ROAD, June 1858, middle-class housing with piped water (24T, 86B). C.S. Brock photographs his wife, his friends and his servants with the family carriage – their transport and status symbol. (105B.)

ST PETER'S CHURCH FLOOR being lowered, November 1858. An exposure of several seconds. Note the workmen's period dress.

PORK BUTCHERS, Middleborough, little concerned about flies, (31) c. 1860. Note the state of the road and the chemist shop next door.

The Town to 1914: Making a Living

RED LION AND STAFF, July 1867. Tudor timbers have been plastered over; there is a shoe shop on the right. Inns were an important part of a market town's economy. A billboard advertises a Friendly Society Fancy Fair at Reed Hall. (62T.)

ELMSTEAD MARKET; Momples Hall stack yard is Colchester-dependent: Harry Smith's portable steam engine driving his thrashing tackle was made by Stanford's in Colchester High Street (87B). Stack yard now occupied by Frating Garage.

WHEATSHEAF PUB, LITTLE BROMLEY, proclaiming Daniell's beers, one of 150 pubs owned by this Colchester family brewery, further evidence of the wide area tied economically to Colchester. Date: 1920s. (90.)

GREENSTEAD WINDMILL in 1899, one of ten still at work in the borough in 1860. Note how this post mill could revolve into the wind on the rail set on its artificial mound. (10T.)

EAST BRIDGE, 1900, outside Marriage's Mill; a carter reads a newspaper beside a heavyweight ladder down which men carry sacks of beans weighing 19 stone each (not recommendable). The building had not yet been transformed into the 'Old Siege House'. (109B.)

MIDDLEBOROUGH, 1899. Saturday livestock market, moved from High Street in 1862; sheep in front, cattle behind, a vital part of the town's life. (89T.)

FRIDAYWOOD FARM, 1878. Note three dogs, four servants and a horse. Colchester borough embraced many rural areas (22). Farmers were prosperous men and central to Colchester's economy.

BENJAMIN CANT (in straw boater) – the best rose grower in England, exhibits his staff and four top national trophies in 1892 (46T). Colchester was famous for roses and horticulture was a significant employer.

THE COLCHESTER EARTHQUAKE revealed much about the poor state of rural housing, April 1884. A builder's gang about to patch up some shattered cottages. (23T.)

LEXDEN VILLAGE, 1890, looking uphill towards The Sun, retained its rural appearance while still providing a home for several of the gentry. (110B.)

FARM WORKERS, Canham, Taylor and Beardwell of Wyncoll's farm, prepare the graveyard of St John's Church, Ipswich Road, another part of the borough still essentially rural, 1905.

DEMOLITION OF ST RUNWALD'S CHURCH, High Street, March 1878. It had a Saxon foundation. The state of the group far right says much about contemporary poverty. (13B.)

OPENING OF SEWAGE WORKS at the Hythe, July 1884, a vital event in the town's history, attended by the mayor, Alfred Francis, and a full muster of borough councillors. (45.)

THE WATER CART, if you could afford it at 1*d.* a bucket, was universal until piped water reached all parts of the borough in the twentieth century.

MOBILE MILKMAN, Charles Perry, crossing East Street; Goody's shop in the background, 1908 (12A, 29B). Before this date poor quality milk was frequently tubercular.

CHURCH COTTAGES, BIRCH, 1905. The lady's new galvanised bucket, brought perhaps by carrier's cart from Colchester market, would have rendered the endless fetching and carrying slightly easier in this apparently idyllic scene.

EAST BAY, 1910. Lucy Hymas's corner shop offers goods on 'tick'. The humble timber-framed shop will soon be dubbed (erroneously) the 'Port Reeve's House'.

HYTHE HILL, St Leonard's Church and the Dolphin in view, 1897. Poverty lurked in hidden courtyards, but humble respectability ruled, despite the 24 pubs or beershops from the Hythe to St Botolph's Corner. (107T, 32.)

THE HYTHE, around 1900. A Newcastle boat has just unloaded its cargo which, to judge from the man with a shovel, was coal. Other men hang around, hoping to pick up casual jobs.

THE HYTHE, BARGES AT REST, 1912. Note the man on the right unloading timber. This exhausting work could involve carrying 15 tons of planks per man per day. Novices' backs became raw and their blood soaked through their shirts.

MR GILMOR, PHOTOGRAPHER, HEAD STREET (near the post office), June 1887. Specialist shops were an important feature of Colchester life and shopkeepers were key citizens.

JOSCELYNE'S CAFE, No. 38 High Street, has a publicity stunt with gentlemen dressed as coffee jars who must have felt complete wallies. The cafe moved in 1930, replaced by Marks & Spencer.

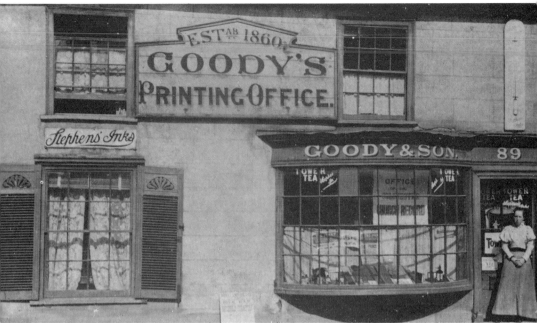

MISS GOODY outside the family business, 1895, little changed since 1856 (12T). In her shop window are copies of *Colchester Church Record* and stone jars of Stephens' ink. She also sells tea. The family shop was one of the few ways Victorian women might run a business. The shop was demolished to build the War Memorial. (84T.)

CO-OPERATIVE STORE, CULVER STREET, east end, Herbert Harding, manager, and staff in 1909. Founded in 1861 for 'the elevation and benefit of the working classes', this, their Central store, included an Assembly Room (far right), the nursery of Colchester's working class Movement. (84B, 124T.)

TALLOW FACTORY, Brook Street, 1900; making candles from animal fat was an important local trade before the incandescent gas-lamp of the 1890s (56T). The rack of wicks is dipped into the tallow.

HEARSUM & COOK'S GAME DISPLAY, Crouch Street, 1913. A fashionable West End street, catering for a Lexden Road clientele. (86B, 120.)

FREDERICK WISE, butcher of High Street, plus staff, makes his contribution to the traditional Christmas display in 1906. His timber-framed shop, demolished in 1989, has been solemnly rebuilt as a modern imitation for Town Hall accommodation. (55).

SEA HORSE INN, east end of High Street, June 1887. Horses are in the stable and drivers are in the bar. Bedwell, upholsterer, is next door (now Markhams). Colchester had 113 licensed premises in 1881, one to every 250 of the population. (26B.)

WILLIAM BRUCE'S COACHWORKS, Middleborough, offers traps for sale, 1900. Small workshops of every sort were more common than factories in Colchester at this date. (16B).

MILL'S COACHWORKS, Childwell Alley, maker of engine-driven delivery vans, 1910. Note the pneumatic tyres on the walls.

STEPHEN BROWN'S SILK MILL, 1878, on the river by Middle Mill (148T), the only big factory in mid-Victorian Colchester, it employed 300 women. Built in 1826, it ceased throwing silk in 1881, but survived as industrial premises until the 1960s.

JOHN KAVANAGH'S BOOT FACTORY, 1890, Stanwell Street, with the entire staff (including many teenagers), built on contract to supply boots to the army (60); the very latest in high tech. and American machinery; sparked Colchester's first real trade union strike, 1892. Later it became Hollington's clothing factory (98B); it was bombed in 1944. (141B.)

MR GEORGE'S BOOT FACTORY, Kendall Road, New Town, with the entire staff, around 1885. Note the contrast between the 'boys' introduced at low wages to run the new machinery and the unionized, skilled men in bowlers. Caught up in the strikes of 1892–5, George sacked all his union men. Later it became Rose's calendar factory.

MOTH & ADAMS, DRESSMAKERS, Trinity Street, 1890. These well-dressed ladies were a social cut above the girls in the silk factory. (44.)

LEANING'S CLOTHING FACTORY, 1913, housed in Knopp's former 'Time Will Tell' Boot Factory at the junction of Mersea and Portland Roads. The notice on the door reads 'Outworkers' Entrance'. (98.)

PAXMAN'S ENGINEERING WORKS was the big employer with over 1,000 men, 1901. This is the large machine shop, heavily capitalized with new machinery, much of which was not used in the lean years that followed. (70B.)

ON BALKERNE HILL, in 1907, the brakes failed as Collier's traction engine towed a truckload of sand downhill (152T). The houses survived, only to be demolished in 1976 when Balkerne Hill was made a dual carriageway.

WORKMEN STREAMING FROM PAXMAN'S in the year of their first strike, 1910, past the office and office staff and an 'Economic' boiler ready for dispatch. (99B.)

MUMFORD'S ENGINEERING in Culver Street, 1909. These premises were initially used by Paxman's. Left to right: Richer, Wright, Mills, Bloomfield, Gosnell and Brown assembling 'Simplex' Pumps. (99T.)

GREAT EASTERN RAILWAY driver, fireman and maintenance men pose with the railway chaplain, 1900. Rather like seamen, railmen boasted their own Mission on North Station Road.

NORTH STATION STAFF pose on the platform in 1898. Note the contemporary advertisements. The horse insisted on being in the picture.

LEVEL CROSSING KEEPERS, Mr Marchant & his wife, at Chitts Hill crossing, May 1885.

BEN NOY, BOILERMAKER and rugged individualist of Back Lane, Hythe, 1903. He walked from Woodbridge to Colchester to get a job; sold Paxman boilers in Prussia; set up on his own; went bust; started again; went bust again. He proudly displays his handiwork in this publicity shot. The chalk writing on the boiler reads: B. NOY, MAKER. (137B.)

THE LOCOMOTIVE STAFF at North station, with the foreman wearing his bowler hat. Railwaymen were central to Colchester's twentieth-century Trade Unionism, providing several early Labour councillors. (115T.)

THE GASWORKS' DAY SHIFT, 1909, shovelled 6 a.m. to 6 p.m., seven days a week, even on Christmas Day, 84 hours a week all year, with only a week's holiday. (96B.)

CHARLES ORFEUR'S BUILDING WORKERS in front of the newly-completed North School, 1894. (122T.)

JUBILEE DAY, June 1887. Customers from the Goat & Boot, East Hill, were still rather wary about cameras. In Victorian Colchester the old, the infirm and women did not always make a living.

The Town to 1914: Public & Social

THE EARLIEST SURVIVING LINE-UP OF COUNCILLORS AND COMMISSIONERS, a roll-call of local businessmen, August 1878. Taken at Hill House, Hythe Hill (now Paxman's Social Club) home of Tommy Moy, mayor, at the opening of the new Hythe Bridge (70T). Left to right: Henry Jones (Jones & Son, solicitors), Nathaniel Cobbold (brewer – at the back), Philip Papillon (squire of Lexden), Bawtree Harvey (chairman, Gas Co.), James Tabor (in front, retired merchant), James Wicks (Wine Merchant – at the back), Alfred Francis (Francis & Gilders, grain merchants), Tom Docwra (farmer), Major Bishop (late of India), John Ward (wearing the hat), John Kent (Kent & Blaxill), Sam Chaplin (miller), Thomas Moy (coal merchant and mayor), Fred Cole (chemist), Tommy Bear (Britannia Engineering), Sayers Turner (town clerk), James Moore (grocer), Francis Smythies (solicitor), Charles Hawkins (Hythe merchant), William Daniell (brewer), Asher Prior (solicitor), William Argent (miller), Brabrook Daniell (farmer), John Lay (Lay & Wheelers) (100T). The sticks they carried were made from the piles of Hythe Bridge of 1406.

COUNCILLORS & OFFICERS IN CASTLE KEEP before it was roofed over, 1891. Left to right, standing: John Bawtree (banker); John Goodey (builder of New Town); Wilson Marriage (miller), A.E. Church (coroner), Will Rampling (town sergeant (with mace)), O. Coombs (chief constable), Dr Brown (medical officer). Seated: Pung Hazell (boot manufacturer), H. Elwes (solicitor), Asher Prior (solicitor), Lent Watts (stonemason and mayor), James Wicks (wine merchant), Ben Cant (rose grower), Brabrook Daniell (farmer). Grounded: H. Goodyear (surveyor), Charles Bland (waterworks).

THE VOLUNTEER FIRE BRIGADE shows off its new steam engine outside the castle, June 1880. Between the wheels stands their chief, James Howe. (74.)

THE PUBLIC LIBRARY, 1894, West Stockwell Street, built by the Town Council after a 40-year debate, did not permit open access. A customer beside the 'Cotgrove Indicator' showing which books are in, asks for one at the counter. The Librarian has the weary look of a public servant. (156.)

BRANCH LIBRARY AT OLD HEATH, 1899, the latest in tin huts, stores newly-felled timber in its small garden.

THE POLICE were an early borough responsi-
bility. 1897, outside No. 21 St Botolph's
Street a constable explains to the Borough
Coroner, Mr Sparling, how the owner, W.C.
Shaw, has hanged himself. (118.)

THE MAYOR, WILSON MARRIAGE (bareheaded) opens Castle Park, October 1892, another
popular civic amenity, guarded by borough police and firemen, led by James Howe. (46B,
74.)

THE BANDSTAND IN CASTLE PARK, 1898, graced by a military band. Note the young trees and the well-dressed young people. A good place for chatting up. (125T.)

A PRAM PROMENADE in Castle Park, 1910. (127B.)

ALBERT SCHOOL OF ART & SCIENCE, 1896, housed in the former Corn Exchange, High Street, became a university extension college. Art classes were attended by some of the best-looking girls in the town. (153B.)

ALBERT SCHOOL again, 1908. Good-looking young men about to sit an evening class drawing exam, inspired by classical sculptures and four staff moonlighting from full-time jobs at Paxman's. (39T.)

THE NEW TECHNICAL SCHOOL, North Hill, 1912, and some of the men who built it, when the Albert School was deemed too decrepit to justify a government grant. The Technical School also housed the Girls' High School. Today it is a Sixth Form College. (153B.)

STAFF OF THE BLUECOAT SCHOOL, St Helen's Lane, 1888. Mr North, headmaster, seated second from left. Note the youthful 'pupil teachers', back right.

TRADITIONAL BLUECOAT SCHOOLBOY, name un-known, wearing his leather breeches, 1880. A Church of England foundation, frosty towards nonconformity; part of its 1855 Gothic buildings still stand in St Helen's Lane.

BLUECOAT SCHOOLGIRLS, traditionally clothed, find it all a bit of a laugh. The uniforms continued to be worn until 1927.

CULVER STREET WESLEYAN SCHOOL TEAM, winners of Colchester Schools Football League, 1901. A Nonconformist school, it fostered devout suspicion of the Church of England. This did not, however, inhibit ferocious use of the cane.

GIRLS OF EAST WARD SCHOOL rehearse a stick dance for the Colchester Pageant, 1908 (72). The coming of Council Schools eased sectarian rivalry and raised educational standards.

MUNICIPAL EXPANSION led to a new Town Hall. In October 1898 Lord Rosebery can just be seen laying the foundation stone. Everyone wore a top hat in the VIP enclosure, guarded by mounted soldiers beside the Angel Inn.

DOWN WITH THE OLD TOWN HALL, 1899. The corporation demolition gang salvages some useful marble.

UP WITH THE NEW TOWN HALL, 1901. A misty morning and a muddy High Street, as wooden scaffolding shrouds the Victoria Tower, named after a Queen just dead, and paid for by James Paxman, just married (101B). Fred Wise's butchers shop is still run by Mr Dennis. (31.)

THE OYSTER FEAST OF 1902, held in the 'new' Corn Exchange. Wilson Marriage, mayor, and some of his 500 guests. Note gas-jet lighting (30T) and paintings of the Oyster Fishery on the wall. Twelve thousand oysters were eaten by the male élite of the district.

COLCHESTER CASTLE was a picturesque ruin, privately owned and unroofed, 1878. There was free parking for carriages on the left and a small museum inside, nationally famous, visited by 15,000 people in 1878. To the right of the fence was the garden of the owner, James Round MP, head of the town's leading family and its senior political figure. (127B.)

GENERAL ELECTION, July 1892. All eyes are on Sir Weetman Pearson, unsuccessful Liberal candidate, driven from High Street in James Paxman's brougham. He was, however, to win the next four elections. (59T.)

THE PUBLIC HALL (later St George's Hall) behind Cullingford's shop in High Street, the headquarters of Colchester Liberalism, June 1897. Four passers-by suspiciously watch the photographer. Note the wine vaults below the pavements, far left. (100T.)

ELECTION ROOMS on North Hill for Worthington Evans, successful Conservative candidate, January 1910. Months later the buildings were removed for the entrance to the new Technical School. (51T.)

TRAM NO. 1, ST BOTOLPH'S STREET, heading for the Hythe a few months after this latest municipal undertaking began, 1908. (68B.)

HEADGATE, A TRIO OF SOLDIERS, perhaps from the Recruiting Office at the corner of Sir Isaac's Walk, 1898. The house at the top of St John's Street was demolished to build the Liberal Club. (143.)

SOLDIERS ON PARADE at the Cavalry Barracks, prior to church parade, following which marching military bands were one of the sights of Colchester.

CHURCH PARADE at Garrison Church (12B). Note the watchful eye of the civil police.

LORD RAGLAN PUB, Military Road, named after the Crimean commander, much frequented by soldiers, 1890s. Note the youthfulness of two of the girls. Other less reputable pubs were often a front for prostitution.

LIFEBOAT SATURDAY 1899 with Friendly Society officials marching by. These were vital organizations among skilled working men. How closely their regalia resembles the socially superior masons.

FREEMASON LINE-UP for the opening of the new Children's Ward at Colchester & Essex Hospital on Lexden Road, 1907. Increasingly masonic membership became desirable for the professionally ambitious.

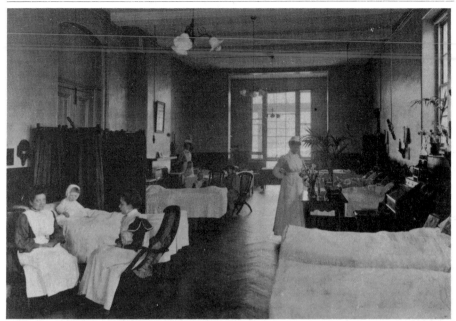

WOMEN'S SURGICAL WARD, COLCHESTER HOSPITAL, 1905. Note the newly-installed electric light. Supported entirely by voluntary donations, the hospital increasingly ran into debt. Only the poor were treated; the wealthy were sick at home.

HEADGATE CHAPEL, 1907. The men's meeting called the Pleasant Sunday Afternoon (PSA), vividly demonstrates the role of religion in Colchester; perhaps 70 per cent of the population attended church. Headgate Chapel is now a restaurant.

CHARLES HADDON SPURGEON (1834–1892), the greatest evangelist of the nineteenth century, probably Colchester's most significant nineteenth-century citizen, lived as a boy on Hythe Hill where his father was clerk to Thomas Moy. (45.)

ARTILLARY STREET CHAPEL, (centre) where, on a snowy morning in 1850, Charles Spurgeón was converted by an unknown preacher. The chapel has since been rebuilt.

ESSEX HALL, the Eastern Counties Asylum For Idiots, built as a railway hotel; turned into a progressive centre for the treatment of the mentally handicapped by the Turner family. In this early, posed photograph, inmates on the left are wearing straight-jackets c. 1870.

WINSLEY'S ALMSHOUSES, Old Heath Road, for 'decayed' men and their wives were, in 1898, retirement homes much sought after. Being a Liberal and a nonconformist greatly helped. The buildings – and homes – remain today.

RISING STANDARDS OF PERSONAL HEALTH are evident in the offer of dentistry for all at this Head Street shop. (86B.)

COLCHESTER'S WORKHOUSE, 1899, last resort of the destitute old was — despite the pot plants, the Master and his staff, snuff on Christmas Day and beer on Saturday — universally dreaded. Popularly called 'The Spike', it was the subject of political scandal when, in the 1870s, it was discovered that the quantity of brandy purchased by the Master greatly exceeded the inmate's medical requirements. It is now St Mary's Hospital.

A SHORT LIFE & MERRY doubtless inspired many a day's outing in horse-drawn brakes, involving a drink or two. Several men wear military uniforms in this 1909 photograph outside Farmer's in High Street. (137T.)

A TRAMTOP VIEW FROM HEADGATE, 1906. A popular family outing was to take the tram to Lexden and back. The less affluent walked there and took the tram back. (143.)

JUBILEE DAY saw universal celebration in Colchester, June 1887. Children under this decorated arch on East Hill lived to see two World Wars. A woman carries yoked buckets.

THE HYTHE BRASS BAND pose in front of the old Hythe railway bridge. Brass bands, religious and secular, flourished at the turn of the century. (121T.)

FAMILY GROUP of James Paxman (left), his son and daughter, fresh from tennis on the lawns of Hill House, once home of Thomas Moy (45). A rich man, Paxman shows suitable respect to his humbly-born, seated relatives, 1885.

BOER WAR VICTORY CELEBRATION, 1902. Paxman foremen Plane and Phillips stand beside a rigged-up traction engine pulling a truck of Paxman 'soldiers'. Paxman's had lost thousands of pounds of orders during the war. (38T.)

ESSEX COUNTY TENNIS CHAMPIONSHIP held at the Lawn Tennis & Croquet Club in Victoria Road, 1911. Mixed Doubles Finals: Colonel Hamilton & Mrs Parker *v*. Captain Parker and Mrs Jenks.

COUNTY CRICKET comes to Castle Park, June 1914. Essex beat Worcester by 193 runs, several of which were made by the Essex captain J.W.H.T. Douglas, seated fourth from left.

THE COLCHESTER PAGEANT induced a high percentage of the middle classes to dress up and declaim, in stilted prose, the town's history, June 1909. This action shot gives some idea of a cast of 3,500.

COLCHESTER PAGEANT, 1909: brutal Vikings being beastly to Saxons, i.e., Mrs Clowes the doctor's wife of Queens Street and her daughter Janet. The Vikings were family friends.

BERECHURCH HALL, 1900. Life's rich pageant in great houses required the labour of Mr Wheeler and Mr Waller chopping wood for 14s. a week to heat a mansion rebuilt by the brewer Octavius Coope in 1881, one of the earliest houses lit by electricity.

BERECHURCH HALL GROUNDS, later owned by the Hetherington family whose son, Thomas Gerald, seen here arriving from Aldershot, was a pioneer aviator, airship enthusiast and co-inventor of the tank. October 1912. (150B.)

JAMES HOWE, IRONMONGER of No. 5 Long Wyre Street and Volunteer Fire Brigade chief, relaxes in his house above his shop, surrounded by the material goods of a successful life: his fireplace, his canary, his vases, his cigar. Every picture tells a story. (46B, 48B).

SUSAN HOWE, HIS WIFE sits much less confidently on the other side of the fireplace. She knows her place and is only glad to have survived eight confinements and the death of one son. Understandably she worries that her children will squabble over the inheritance. They did.

MARSHALL HOWE, SON OF JAMES, outside the family shop in Long Wyre Street, described in a Trade Guide as 'a capital frontage thirty feet of which is occupied by windows for the display of goods of all description, among which may be mentioned baths, travelling trunks, kitchen ranges, wire netting, cutlery, electro-plated goods, garden seats, bird cages, chandeliers, guns and ammunition'. It was also a locksmiths, gasfitters, bell-hangers and gunsmiths.

SECTION FOUR

War & After: 1914–1920

MEN OF THE RAMC IPSWICH TERRITORIALS pass through Colchester High Street in the first week of the First World War, August 1914. Note the *Essex County Standard* Office back right.

A ZEPPELIN OVER COLCHESTER. Frequently seen in daylight, on one occasion five were overhead simultaneously. One crash-landed at Great Wigborough and souvenirs from it still exist in Colchester families.

GORDON HIGHLANDERS MARCHING down Pownell Crescent. At times in the war Colchester had more soldiers than civilians, a severe strain on food supplies. The Gordon Highlanders were a severe strain on pubs.

THE FIRST WOUNDED SOLDIERS arriving at St Botolph's station, a newspaper reporter taking notes, October 1914. Up to 15,000 wounded were handled by the Military Hospital, the Essex County (63T), Hamilton Road School and a large house in Cambridge Road. Local women produced 25,546 bandages.

PAXMAN'S SECRET WAR WORK included the construction of these early paravanes for dealing with mines at sea.

STONES ENGINEERING, erstwhile garage owners, whose staff of 12 made army munitions. Mr Stone is seated.

PAXMAN'S MUNITION WORKERS included 400 women in 1916. Ann Stevens, second left, became an instructor despite losing a finger in an accident. 'We were all happy doing work for our country', she recalled 70 years later.

QUEUEING FOR POTATOES, December 1917, and indeed for everything, became normal; the mayor had to commandeer butter to prevent a riot.

80,000 RATION CARDS being written by hand in the Moot Hall by 180 borough schoolteachers, February 1918. Schools were closed for a week and the cards delivered by boy scouts.

FIRST WOMAN TRAM CONDUCTRESS, Ann Cuddon, checking the wind direction, 1916. Mr Buller, tramway manager, looks distinctly upstaged.

ESSEX YEOMANRY MOTOR VOLUNTEER CORPS (Coast Section), on parade. Centre, Frederick Bird, landlord of the Plough Hotel, St Botolph's Corner. (94B.)

COMBINED CHOIRS processing up Mersea Road from St Giles Church, 1918. Christianity took on a public fervour as Britain came close to defeat, but suffered a loss of support after the war. (121B.)

MARCH PAST THE NEW WAR MEMORIAL, 1924, built despite a rival proposal for an art gallery. An officer looks round to check the men are still there. (12T.)

MAY DAY MARCH past the new garage (left) in Queen Street, built by National Steam Car Co. on the site of the burnt-down theatre, by banner-carrying Trades Council and Labour Party, 1920. In the hard years after the war the Labour Party grew. The garage is now a bus station.

Colchester Between the Wars: 1920–1939

MOTOR MECHANICS and the body building division of H.J. Willet, High Street, prior to the Ford Motor Exhibition, October 1935. Inter-war Colchester saw the rise of the motor car, a symbol of rising living standards, but the preserve of the few. (104, 105, 109, 110.)

ELEGANT HOUSES IN THE AVENUE (this is No. 2) frequently housed army officers. In No. 7 in 1883 the future Field Marshal Earl Wavell was born. Note the croquet hoops.

MR MARGETSON, DENTIST, offers from his house, No. 119 Crouch Street, a service to the affluent West End of Colchester. Rooms where artificial teeth were made today house an Indian Restaurant.

ALBION COURT behind Long Wyre Street, 1928, was demolished for a shopping arcade. Nothing of architectural merit was lost.

BACK LANE, HYTHE (now Spurgeon Street), 1928. The photographer rightly deemed it a prime example of a slum and carefully posed the occupants. Note the outside loo.

SHRUB END COTTAGE of traditional weatherboard and thatch, picturesque but perhaps uncomfortable, 1934. This one stood just beyond All Saints' Church. (8T.)

JOHN DEATH, COAL MERCHANT, trades from his house on Magdalen Street, 1925. Cork over the doorway is both trade mark and merchandise, the whitened step a mark of respectability. Miss Death was full of life.

FENN WRIGHT'S HORSE AUCTIONS sometimes brought wild gypsies to the town. The men in this 1923 photograph, however, are all 'good old boys'.

EMPLOYEES OF STAMFORD, engineers, High Street. More good old boys, off for a boozy outing to West Mersea on Berry's bus, 1920s. (68T.)

ROSE & CROWN, EAST GATE, unrestored, offers whisky, gin and accommodation for cyclists, 1920s. Note the billboard advertising the Hippodrome and the ever-present Daniell & Son, Brewers. (18B.)

THE HOMEMADE BREAD CO., Long Wyre Street, with Lil Spack and a friend ready to serve you in the restaurant upstairs, 1922. The bakery was at the back where, during the First World War, apples were dyed in cochineal to make fruit cake constituents.

BERT MOORE, former milkman (left), stands with his assistant outside his cycle shop in North Station Road, June 1925. Posters advertise the East of England Championship.

THE DELIVERY CART of Blomfield's, ironmongers of St Botolph's Street, with the three children of Mr Chatters who drove it, outside their house in Winchester Road. (143.)

DELIVERY VAN of Wrights, Coal Merchants, Hythe. Right, Mr Albert Wright, left, his assistant Albert Brown. (141B.)

LEFT: DELIVERY BOY, PELHAM'S LANE, passes the warehouse of Burton, Son & Sanders, wholesale grocers. Right: D.W. Jeffery, jewellers, of High Street employed Mr Mills to drive this Humber motorbike round the district winding up watches and clocks. (c 1914.)

TIME TO BUY A CLOCK at the Co-op Jewellery Department, 1928. (29B.)

PROMOTIONAL VAN OF CHESHIRE'S, China Stores, St Botolph's Street, driven by Ted Frost at the Colchester Carnival. Note the firm's brief telephone number. (116.)

FREDDY BIRD, LANDLORD OF THE PLOUGH, St Botolph's Corner, demonstrates to spectators at the Colchester Rose Show the purpose of the Beer Tent, 1921. His son looks on. (83T, 105B.)

E.N. MASON'S DISPLAY at the Colchester Empire Exhibition, July 1930. Founded by the remarkable Mrs Mason in 1905, the firm made office equipment and pioneered photo-copying. Her son, Bernard Mason, opened a new model factory on the bypass. (133.)

GRAMMAR SCHOOL FUND RAISING OLD ENGLISH FAIR in aid of proposed memorial swimming pool (still in use), 1923. Left, headmaster, H.J. Cape, plus several masters' wives, fixing potential customers with their beady eyes.

COLCHESTER GAS COMPANY'S NEW PREMISES in Head Street being given their finishing touches, September 1931. Luckin Smith occupied an identical shop next door. (9, 43T.)

DIRECTORS OF THE GAS COMPANY, 1937. Clockwise: Mr Lugley (secretary), Sam Blomfield, S. Daniell, Thompson Smith, V. Marshall, Gerald Benham (chairman), Mr Smith (manager) – a contrast with the day shift. (43T.)

W. GURNEY BENHAM, owner and editor of the *Essex County Standard*, mayor, alderman and savant, in his editor's lair, represents 'the boss', autocratic but paternalistic, that characterized the family businesses of Colchester. 1931.

COMPOSITORS AT BENHAMS, PRINTERS, checking the small print, in poor gas light, for the *Essex County Standard*, 1931.

CUTTERS AT HYAMS, CLOTHIERS, Abbeygate Street, the aristocrats of the rag trade, 1931. All men.

GIRLS AT HOLLINGTONS, CLOTHIERS, Stanwell Street, hunched over sewing machines, supervized by their foremen and paid piece rates. Needles often went through their fingers. (37B.)

THE CLOSURE OF MUMFORDS, ENGINEERS, August 1933. A six-wheel lorry squeezes out of Culver Street into Head Street taking away machinery leaving hundreds of men out work. (39B, 157.)

PAXMAN'S SURVIVES, based on new diesel engines and old economic boilers, seen here under construction, 1938. The working conditions and the plant are little changed since 1900. (38T.)

LAY & WHEELER'S WINE VAULT, 1923, under High Street (58B), contains port bottled in 1855 by John Lay, founder of this family firm. (45).

WOODS ENGINEERING, founded 1909, a rising firm, moved to works in Denmark Street. Seen here in the Winding Shop are coils being wound on armatures, 1930s.

WOODS SPECIALIZED IN FANS from 1933, employing 200 staff by 1935. An early view of the test section, with polishing motors, starters and fans on view.

THE TOWN HALL, 1934, looming over a public toilet, an early telephone box and the head of the taxi rank (105T), was also a considerable employer.

NEW ELECTRICITY WORKS OPENED at the Hythe in October 1927. Left, Charles Smallwood, Colchester's first Labour mayor, keen promoter of the scheme; centre, Colchester's first lady mayor, Mrs Alderton. A table lamp proves it all actually works.

CORPORATION DUST CART in its Osborne Street home, 1935.

THE MODERN WONDERS OF ELECTRICITY. Left: this 1905 power-driven hair brush at Richard's in Head Street still worked in 1949. Right: The first Colchester telephone kiosk, 1925: officials explaining how to flush it.

BOROUGH HOUSING DEPARTMENT'S EARLY LORRY (a Morris one-tonner) with driver Claude Theobald (111B) during the building of St Anne's Road Estate, 1927. Note the back wheel.

THE AMATEURS, 1898. On Good Friday Oliver Peck and L. Wash drove their early motor car to Kelvedon High Street and back. A new era had dawned.

ADAMS, COACHBUILDERS, (established in 1848) successfully convert to motor engineers, parking their old van outside their new garage in Culver Street (East), February 1936.

THE PROFESSIONALS, 1921. Old Mr Goslin (right) owner of one of the first taxis on the High Street rank, a site earlier used by hansom cabs (101B), founded the Red Garage in Crouch Street, with his son (left).

PRIDE OF OWNERSHIP exudes from Freddy Bird (left) (94B), posed with his wife's Ford car, all set for an outing to Southend, 1925. (15B.)

LOST COLCHESTER: Osborne Street, July 1931. The building right, was once St Botolph's Brewery, then Griffin's Furniture Store (140T); the building, centre, on the corner of Arthur Street, the Womens' Help Society, is about to be demolished. Note the bicycles.

CHANGING COLCHESTER, 1927: St John's Street, looking east (2B); not a car in sight, only a farmer with his colt.

TRACTION ENGINE ACCIDENT, at the bottom of Hythe Hill, 1927. The flywheel had shot off. The cart is waiting to take the injured man to hospital. A girl talks to the horse.

MOTOR CAR ACCIDENT in Barrack Street opposite Wimpole Road, 1933. A policeman takes notes. The other car is off the picture, right.

THE NEW BUS PARK, St John's Street, 1926, paved in concrete, a modern wonder, doubtless to cope with solid-tyred, open-deck buses.

HISTORIC BUILDINGS about to be demolished to enlarge the bus park, 1927. Wormell's charabancs started from here.

HARWICH ROAD, BOTTOM, wet road; an Eastern Counties bus heads for the level crossing. The destination board reads: Drury Hotel via Butt Road.

EAST BRIDGE BEING WIDENED, November 1927. All traffic passed here going to and from Ipswich or to and from the coast from London. Traffic jams grew. At Whitsun 1932 28,000 vehicles passed over this bridge. (19B.)

HEAD STREET full of motor traffic, 1930 (96T); only the LNER delivery waggon uses a horse. This too is the main route to Ipswich and the coast. The answer is a bypass.

LEXDEN SPRINGS, a traditional Colchester beauty spot, immortalized in this Edwardian photograph, was, with public regret, breached by the bypass.

BYPASS BUILDING at the Glen, Lexden, August 1930. A light railway hauls 173 one-ton waggons to cart the soil away.

BYPASS DIESEL LOCO at Sheepen Road driven by Claude Theobald whose dog Bonzo carried a red flag in his teeth to stop the traffic and got his photograph in the *Daily Mirror*. (103B.)

BYPASS BRIDGE over the River Colne used reinforced concrete for Britain's first two-hinged arch bridge, June 1931. Workmen lay the reinforcing. Below a bathing pool is being built.

BYPASS AT HARWICH ROAD, October 1930, looking towards the future St Andrew's Avenue (9B). To relieve unemployment digging was done by hand by over 1,000 local men.

LORD ULLSWATER OPENS THE BYPASS, dressed in topper and tails, after shaking hands with unemployed workers dressed in working clothes, June 1933.

BYPASS OPEN, Lexden end, deserted but for two girls and a dog, July 1933. Today, despite the traffic, this view is still unspoilt.

CIVIC CEREMONY surrounds Colchester's famous oysters. Here, in 1915, off Brightlingsea, the Fishery steamer *Pyefleet* transports the entire council, like Stanford's workmen, (89B) for an annual booze-up: the Opening of the Oyster Fishery.

OYSTERS. Left: 1931 Mayor Will Harper, sports shop owner, dredges the first oysters. Right: 1930 Mayor Chris Jolly and Town Clerk Hiscott taste the first oysters, a 'tradition' invented in 1913 by press photographers.

MAYOR CHRIS JOLLY, engine driver, leads three cheers for the king, September 1930. Note the gin on the table. Town clerk Hiscott's glasses glint with patriotic intensity.

A PATRIOTIC WELCOME FOR THE PRINCE OF WALES, October 1931. Accompanied by Mayor Harper, the future Edward VIII, visiting Colchester to attend the Oyster Feast (56), inspects girl guides in Castle Park. (49.)

CIVIC FUNERAL for Alderman Cheshire (94T) coming from St Botolph's Church, 1923 (140T). The police sergeant's right turn signal is watched by Colonel Stockwell, chief constable, who is behind in a cocked hat. Note the police war medals.

ALDERMAN CHESHIRE'S FUNERAL CORTÈGE travels down Mersea Road to the cemetery. Funerals were never the same when they used cars.

FUNERAL OF A FIREMEN, killed at a fire in George Street, 1928. The wreath-hung fire engine forms a bier, slowly moving up Mersea Road in the shadow of the Abbey Wall. (15T, 46B.)

A MILITARY FUNERAL in New Town, the coffin mounted on a gun carriage, a familiar Colchester sight. (134T.)

COLCHESTER POLICE FORCE, stepping out at their annual inspection, impelled forward by the glares of the inspecting officers, 1920s.

COLNE RIVER POLICE guarding the Oyster Fishery, 1920s. One feels they could use a rather faster vessel. (114T.)

GREENSTEAD ROAD SCHOOL, 1910: 51 in the class, banked up in rows, facing the teacher-preacher, seen but not heard.

NEW CHURCH SCHOOL, Maldon Road, pioneering new attitudes to children: 10 in the classroom, relaxed and individual, sitting at tables where they can talk, 1928.

HOMEWOOD HOUSE SCHOOL, Lexden, their first three pupils, April 1922. Private schools flourished and new ones arose, mostly at the West End of town.

ST MARY'S SCHOOL, Lexden Road, annual photograph, 1926. During the inter-war period boys attended the junior section of this girls' school.

THE SALVATION ARMY, 1920s, lined up with band in St John's Avenue outside their citidal, a converted ice rink, which had witnessed dramatic Victorian evangelism. A family organization, drawn from the humbler classes.

MUSCULAR CHRISTIANITY, 1938. St Peter's Young Men's Bible Class gymnastic team, winners of the Ganzoni Shield 1937, 1938, 1939. Churches continued to be a focus for such social activity.

OLD COLCHESTER SWIMMING POOL, 1920, Colne Bank Avenue, before the bypass open-air pool was built. North School girls take the plunge. (43B.)

GROUP FROM COLCHESTER SWIMMING CLUB, taken at the open-air swimming pool, 1930s. The club was founded in 1884, swimming at 'Barnes's Place' in the River Colne.

LAYER ROAD, ground of Colchester Town Football Club, then in Spartan League, October 1934. Players and Committee observe a minute's silence on death of Charles Clark, secretary and driving force for many years. (154, 155.)

ESSEX SCHOOLS FOOTBALL CHAMPIONSHIP FINAL, Hamilton Road School, Colchester versus an East Ham school, which ended in a goalless draw, 1925. Mayor Dame Catherine Hunt presents the cup to both captains. Alderman Blaxill, holding his hat, is delighted.

CO-OPERATIVE DAY in Coichester, July 1924, with a procession of floats illustrating the Society's products, parading through New Town from the local Branch. (12B, 29B.)

ANNUAL CARNIVAL PROCESSION in Mersea Road, August 1930. (117T). A horse bus loaned from London preceeds a corporation bus; boy scouts collect. The Carnival grew out of the Hospital Saturday collections. (63T.)

YMCA GALA DAY, Castle Park July, 1931. A wise guy, four dolls and a bored ice-cream man. (127B, 149B.)

CUPS & TROPHIES at the Tramways Department Flower Show held in the Corn Exchange, 1927. The Mayor, Ernest Turner, is seated third right, Charles Smallwood, Deputy Mayor, second right. (102T.)

VAUDEVILE CINEMA, Mersea Road, with staff publicizing Charlie Chaplin's *Gold Rush*, February 1926. Renamed the Empire in 1927; demolished for St Botolph's roundabout, 1971.

THE EMPIRE PUBLICITY TEAM for *The Flag Lieutenant* starring Anna Neagle, 1932. Their Penny Rushes on Saturday morning attracted hundreds of children.

SHOCKING GOINGS ON in Colchester's new Repertory Theatre's first production, *The Late Christopher Bean*, performed in the Albert Hall, High Street, the former Corn Exchange, Technical School and Art Gallery, October 1937. (50T, 84T.)

ROMAN COLCHESTER, March 1932. Excavations in front of the castle uncover the temple entrance. Archaeology had a high profile in intellectual Colchester. Digging was not then done by students. (57.)

CHARABANC OUTING for Hills & Son, builders, begins outside their yard in Pownell Crescent 1920s. (68T.)

OUTING TO LONDON ZOO for girls of Hyam's factory, all equipped with saucy hats, 1920s. (98.)

HYAM'S GIRLS AND COACHES outside the milk bar opposite the bus park prior to an outing to Clacton, 1936. The transport has changed significantly in 16 years.

COLCHESTER MOTOR CLUB MEMBERS set out for the Eastern Counties Trials from F. Metcalf's, next door to Jeffery, jewellers, in the High Street. (93T.)

TECHNICAL SCHOOL, OLD BOYS DINNER, 1931. (51T.) At this date the 'old school tie' was more than a cliché. Note the stuffed shirts.

LAW CLERKS' DINNER in Nuttall's Oak Hall, 1930s. Note the string quartet being deferential to the deferential.

CHRISTMAS PARTY amid the sewing machines at Hollington's Clothing Factory, 1920s. Note the gas lighting. (98B.)

CORONATION STREET PARTY in Charles Street, 1937. Lots of tea and sandwiches. (149T.)

QUOITS TEAM, Station Hotel, Wivenhoe, 1920s. A popular male recreation, quoits was based on the ubiquitous pub.

ESSEX & SUFFOLK FOXHOUNDS meet at the Leather Bottle, Shrub End, February 1930. (8T). Ind Coope beers are on sale close to Berechurch Hall. (73T, 150B.)

Colchester at War: 1939–46

DAD'S ARMY 1943. Part of E.N. Mason's platoon of the Home Guard on the steps of Mason's new factory, the Arclight Works, built off Cowdray Avenue on the 1933 bypass (112). Mason's platoon saw real action when the Arclight Works received a direct hit in October 1942. During the war the firm produced, *inter alia*, 46,140 miles of blueprint and photographic paper, 60,000 camera mountings for bombers and a million and a quarter bottles of ink in their contribution to photo reconnaissance.

COLCHESTER BARRACKS, and the 24th Field Battalion is still not mechanized in 1936. Note the commander's car in the background. When the war came the horses were put down.

ST GEORGE'S DAY SERVICE. Councillors and military walk two by two up Stanwell Street, led by Alderman Piper. (142B.) Their small talk does not suggest impending war.

COLCHESTER'S SATURDAY STREET MARKET: business as usual as Chamberlain becomes Prime Minister and appeasement begins, June 1937.

A SAND-BAGGED SHELTER at Joslin's the Ironmongers, High Street, 1938. Mr Bareham is on guard; the photographer is inexperienced.

VOLUNTEERS FILLING SAND-BAGS at the local gravel pits, 1939. Smoking in front of the lorry is Rex Hull, the museum curator.

THE TOWN HALL BESIEGED BY SAND-BAGS, 1940. The sign on the lamp-post (left) says: AIR RAID SHELTER.

MEN SETTING UP STALLS outside St Nicholas' Church, 1940. (2, 134B, 158.) A smart car can be seen outside Farmer's. (68T.)

MAIDENBURGH STREET, 1940. The Dutch Quarter looks 'unhistoric'. The engineering shed on the right was the last venture of Ben Noy. (41B.)

ST BOTOLPH'S CORNER, 1940: a milk cart being chased by a lorry. To the left is the entrance to Griffin's Furniture Depository (141); after that Stanwell Street. (106T.)

PRIORY STREET 1940, looking east. A woman studies her neighbour's curtains. These houses are all now demolished to reveal the Roman Wall behind.

VINEYARD STREET, 1940, now demolished for car parking. War-time local transport and Colchester-made cast iron railings can be seen, soon to be taken for 'salvage'.

SCHEREGATE STEPS, 1940, looking unromantic; the soldier in the shadow carries a rifle. The arrow on the lamp-post (striped because of the blackout) says: AIR RAID SHELTER. (6T.)

BOMBING OF SEVERALL'S MENTAL HOSPITAL caused 63 casualties, August 1942.

SMOKE HANGS OVER SITE OF BLOMFIELD'S, Ironmongers, destroyed, as were three factories and fourteen properties, in a fire bomb raid on St Botolph's Corner, 24 February 1944. (35, 37B, 92T, 138T.)

ST BOTOLPH'S CHURCH stands above the ruins of the Britannia Engineering Works, another victim of the incendiaries, February 1944. Fire Guards and two schoolboys saved the church. (116T.)

WRIGHT'S LORRIES helping to clear the wreckage at the Britannia Works, February 1944. (92B, 144B.)

HIGH-SPIRITED AUSTRALIAN TROOPS were based in Colchester from October 1940. (This photograph at the Cavalry Barracks is probably of pre-war British soldiers with an Australian flag. Can any reader help?)

AMERICAN AIRMEN gave parties to children and a silver bowl to Alderman Piper, the mayor 1944–45. No photograph survives of their other activities.

WAR-TIME HEADGATE, 1944. A Red Cross van swings into Head Street where bombed-out Blomfield's have been rehoused under the Liberal Club. Bicycles predominate; coupons are needed for shopping. (60T, 140B.)

AN OPEN-AIR SERVICE outside Paxman's office; choir centre, Works Committee on platform, 1945. Ted Paxman is the third from right, Percy Sanders, fifth. (39T, 93B.)

ASSEMBLING PAXMAN T.P. VEE ENGINES, 1943, at the Britannia Works prior to the fire bombs of 1944. Note the mostly women workers. (80B, 141T.)

WOMEN EMERGING FROM THE SHELTER in front of the castle to which so many arrows pointed, enjoying a joke, 1944. Shephard's Funeral Services is in the background. (136B, 139B.)

PATRIOTIC FLOWER BED in Castle Park, 1939.

PEACE with VICTORY
COLCHESTER THANKS YOU

LEST WE FORGET how close two World Wars were to one another here (July 1919) and on the next page are the victory celebrations, after both those wars, so similar in sentiment, saluting the glorious dead, outside Colchester Town Hall.

THE ESSEX REGIMENT marches through Colchester, bayonets fixed, colours flying, bands playing, as part of the victory celebrations, May 1946. No such military march past has happened since.

MIDDLE MILL and a frozen river during a bitter winter, February 1945. Youngsters make slides; PC49 looks approvingly on. Not a punk in sight (34).

FITNESS WINS THE WAR, prophetically proclaimed by these St Helena schoolgirls in a war-time carnival, 1942.

A STREET PARTY for Foresight Road combined with the residents of Speedwell Road, Old Heath, May 1945. At least 60 such parties were held in Colchester.

WE'LL EAT AGAIN. Miss Cassell, aged 15, sells Ward's ice-cream coupon-free in Harwich Road, 1946. Ward's refrigerator was serviced by Mr Newcombe who met and married Miss Cassell. This caption is dedicated to them. Note the slogan on the bus.

GERMAN PRISONERS (in the First World War) being marched to West Mersea Church for a service.

BERECHURCH HALL MILITARY CORRECTIVE TRAINING CENTRE, built to house German prisoners of war, became the much-dreaded Colchester 'glasshouse' during National Service days.

Post-War Colchester

COLCHESTER'S NEW PUBLIC LIBRARY photographed in the 1950s, was two-thirds complete on the eve of the war, served as Food Office for the duration, finally opening as a library in 1947 (156). The spire of Lion Walk and the tower of St Botolph's pierce the sky (140T). The car park is beginning to fill up with more and more private cars. . . .

COLLIER'S BRICKYARDS, Marks Tey, continued its labour-intensive, handmade brick-making long after this Edwardian photograph. (38B.)

MOLAR WORKS at the Hythe, 1950s, whose mass production of bricks grew on the back of the post-war housing drive.

WOOD'S NEW FACTORY at Braiswick, 1949, built 1938, extended 1944, symbolizes the modernization of Colchester engineering in the 1940s and 1950s. Note the steam train and eight parked cars.

TECHNICAL EDUCATION 1951. The entire staff of North-East Essex Technical College, North Hill. Today their Sheepen Road staff numbers over 300 and North Hill is a sixth form college. (51T.)

HIGH TECH HITS LAYER ROAD, home of Colchester United Football Club, as players try out the new Heading Machine, 1950.

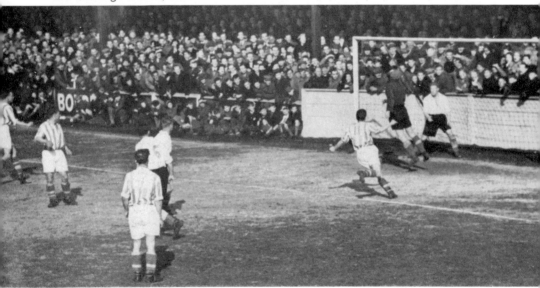

SPOT THE BALL, 1950. U's *versus* Watford, Colchester scores. The crowd is so large they spill over the barrier to sit in an orderly row.

MUD FLIES as Colchester play Plymouth Argyll, March 1951. (123T.)

CUP TIE AGAINST ARSENAL, 1959; dreams of giant-killing. Laurie Honeyball of *Essex County Newspapers* (second right) squats with representatives of the national dailies.

LIBRARY STAFF pose for the last time outside their 1894 building next to the Town Hall, October 1947. Front row: Mr Boulter; Mr Austing, borough librarian; Miss Gosnell; Ronald Blythe, noted author; Miss Cook; Mr Cole.

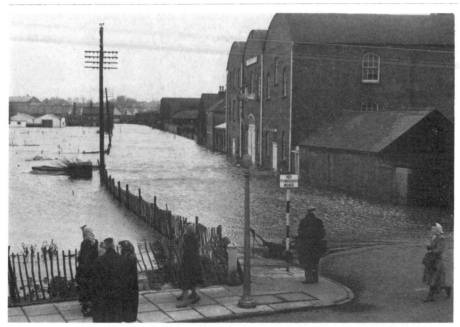

EAST COAST FLOODING at Hawkins Road, Hythe, February 1953. 'No Through Road' it says.

YOUNG MARGARET ROBERTS of Cambridge Road, Colchester, chubby and cheerful, dances the night away with Bill Joliffe, fellow Young Conservative, 1949. Seeking to be MP for Dartford, she met and married Dennis Thatcher. The rest is history.

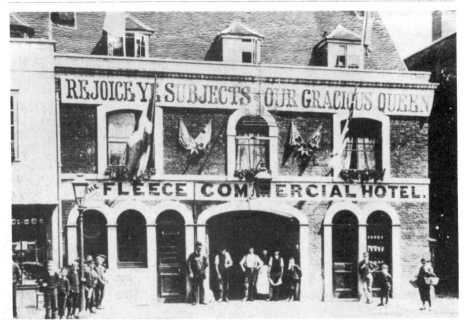

DEVELOPMENT NEVER STOPS. The Fleece Hotel, a timber building, recalls Colchester's ancient cloth trade. From 1887 (top) to 1956 (bottom) it saw several changes, only to be demolished in 1970.